Ducks

by Ruth Mattison

Pioneer Valley Educational Press, Inc.

Here is a duck.
A duck is a bird.

Look at the beak.

beak

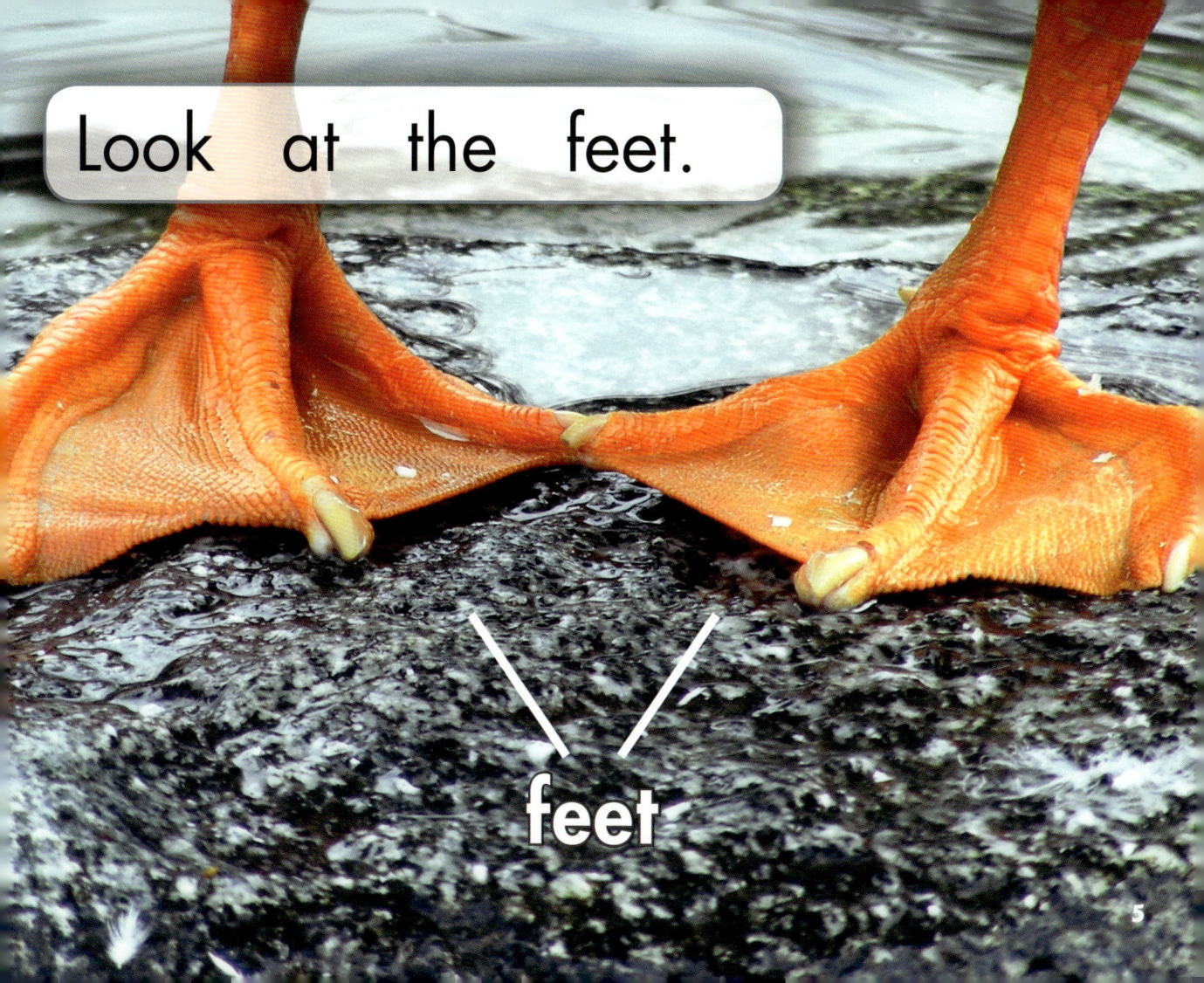

Look at the feet.

feet

Here is a baby duck.
A baby duck is a duckling.

7

A duck can swim.
Look at the duck swimming.

My family helps people.

9

A duck can fly.
Look at the duck flying.

11

beak

duckling

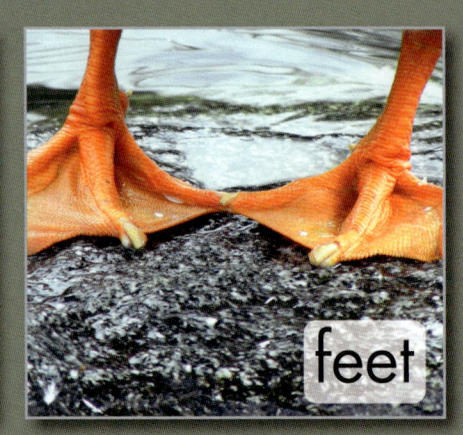

feet

flying

swimming